*Picture a Gate Hanging Open
and Let that Gate be the Sun*

*Picture a Gate Hanging Open
and Let that Gate be the Sun*

poems by
Jerry Mirskin

MAMMOTH books
DuBois, Pennsylvania

Copyright © 2002 Jerry Mirskin

All rights reserved. No part of this book may be reproduced in any manner without written permission from the publisher, except for brief quotations used in reviews or critical articles.

MAMMOTH books
7 Juniata Street
DuBois, Pennsylvania 15801

info@mammothbooks.com
www.mammothbooks.com

The cover's angel image by Charles Sorlier after Chagall
Assistance with the cover design provided by
    Fred Estabrook and Dan Meeker
Author photo by Eric Brooks
Book design by MAMMOTH books
Production by Daamen, Inc.

ISBN 0-9666028-9-7
Library of Congress Catalog Card Number: 2001118994

First Edition

Acknowledgements

The following poems have appeared in *Ascent, Camellia, MSS., New Myths, Paintbrush, Prairie Schooner, The Greenfield Review, The Madison Review, The Seneca Review,* or *14850:*
"Abandoning a Car in Brooklyn, The Thing About Angels," "Adam & Eve," "Bronx Park East," "Cyclops," "Deer," "End of the Season," "Early in the Book of Brothers and Sisters," "Fiesole," "Grace," "Grandmother," "Geese," "Gulls," "Happiness," "Icarus," "Islamorada," "Joe, 2 a.m.," "Noah," "Swimmer," "The Falls," "The Tree," and "Thirty."

The poem "Rock and Water" appeared on-line at www.pith.net.
The poem "My Father" appeared in the *Anthology of Magazine Verse & Yearbook of American Poetry.*
The poems "Bronx Park East" and "My Father" appeared in *Roots and Flowers.*
The poems "Bronx Park East," "Happiness," "Early in the Book of Brothers and Sisters," and "Grace" appeared in *The Prairie Schooner Anthology of Contemporary Jewish American Writing.*
The poems "Deer" and "Rock and Water" appeared in Cayuga Nature Center's Commemorative Chapbook, *Thaw and Flood.*
The poems "Abandoning a Car in Brooklyn, The Thing About Angels," "Adam & Eve," "Cyclops," "End of the Season," "Fiesole," "Grandmother," "Geese," "Gulls," "Icarus," "Noah," and "The Tree" were published together as a chapbook by Camellia Press, Inc.

I would like to acknowledge my spirit teachers:
Dr. Theodore Steinberg, who cast the spell of literature.
Robert Zappulla, who taught the art of work.
Milton Kessler for song.
Robert Mooney and Jeff Schiff for brotherhood.
Irving and Harriet Mirskin for capacious love.
Joanna and Maupi, David and Liz, Jack and Ann, Vicky Anderson, and David Wasson for sustenance.
I would also like to thank David Weiss
for his insightful comments.
And, finally, I would like to thank Antonio Vallone
for his effort on behalf of this manuscript and those of many others.

for Noah and Wendy

for Patricia Flery and Tomer Inbar

Contents

One

15	Seasonal Work
16	Fiesole
17	Geese
18	Thirty
19	Icarus
20	The Last of the Snow
21	Adam & Eve
22	Gulls
23	Early in the Book of Brothers and Sisters
25	Deer
26	Absence
27	Eastport
28	Peninsula State Park
29	Spring Song
30	The Tree

Two

33	The Comet
34	Cyclops
35	Swimmer
36	Dream After Birth
37	This Year the Water
38	There Were Times
39	Joe, 2 a.m.
40	Abandoning a Car in Brooklyn, The Thing About Angels
41	End of the Season
43	Islamorada
45	Nature
46	Bell Tower

48	Siena
49	Manhattan Bridge
50	Bronx Park East
52	Genesis
53	Dear Mozart
54	The Falls

Three

57	Happiness
59	My Father
60	Prayer Shawl
61	You are the Hero
63	Homage
65	Noah
67	Grandmother
69	Holocaust Memorial, Baltimore, Maryland
71	Grace
73	Rock and Water

One

Seasonal Work

The field was bare and dry.
We stood up once an hour
to turn the sled at the end of the row.
The rest of the time we sat peacefully
carefully adding our bundles of grape shoots to the field.
The five of us telling stories,
what we liked to drink, how we spent last night.
The tractor moved slow as growth.
Four sitting, and the one standing
methodically placing another bundle in our laps.
The work was done mostly with the hands.
Sitting shoulder to shoulder
we pressed the earth between plow open
and plow close. Pressing
with our small fingers of life.

I think I remember that warm plow cut,
our four hands in the earth, putting in a word
and then another.
I think I remember our communal hands.
How they grew rough and dry as God's.
And how the driver called to us to *Go to planting*.
I remember that. His voice still hangs on a limb.

Seasonal work.
That was a good dream.
The next might be better, or worse.
Maybe next time I will have wings
and look down from above.
My hands no longer in the earth.

Fiesole

I like the way they live forever in Italy.
I like the way they take the time to do it.
How they put their whole lives into it.
The wine will tell you this.
The way it stands on the table.
So lonely, dark and lonely.
I like the way they live forever in Italy.
Like each day they put a penny in.
A penny for art. One for work.
They know it will take a whole life to pay off.
All this art. All this beauty.
In Fiesole, outside of Florence
I saw two men walking the hills.
When they passed a small faded shrine
their walk faded. They gave a few pennies.
A handful of lira.
They were on one side of a hill
walking a small path to their homes.
On the other side was the city, and the duomo.
You can see it ten miles away
like a great tired heart sleeping soundly
in the smoke of sunlight.
Asleep and snug in the valley by the Arno.
Which side would I prefer?
From here we could see that the sun
was going down on one knee.
The grooves of the city were growing taller
like a taller garden.
Shadows were growing clever in the alleys.
Still, the sun was working hard as always.
Conspiring with the church and the city on one side
and the vine on the other.
I like the way they live forever in Italy.

Geese

One time I was in love
with a little tree. It was winter,
the tree had wandered out of Christmas
and ended up in a window
in the ice where fishermen wait
hours in the cross-eyed cold
for the fish too big to imagine
to pass out of the lake
and nose by them like a cloud.
I spent a lot of time nuzzling
the small blue fans of my tree
and hugging it for the kindling
of its shivery blue breath.
Together we waited for the stars.
The first ones with their wonderful memories
and then the majors and the minors
to pitch and burn all night
with a light as hard as wheat.
It was one of those times we saw geese.
Six white geese, flying in the deep of the sky,
a straight line for the future.
I remember wondering if they were the same
as those I had seen a few years before
flying over a friend's wedding
just as they were pushing their fingers
through the rings. Being in love
I waved for them to come down
come and be with us, but they wouldn't
and continued flying, as if all they were ever
going to have is the dark. And in that way
were like real gods. And in that way
required nothing from us.

Thirty

My friend the bird
who crashed into my house
died wings open in the grass
while the sun was healing
both of us.

The patterns of the constellations
are getting older. As I get older
they're easier to see—

They're all the shapes of cars.

Sometimes this year I notice
as I walk around, putting one foot
firmly in front of the other,
that I'm so used to everything

I hear traffic in the dark
and in the distance light honking.

Thirty years old and this one discovery.

Icarus

To understand this story
you have to picture a gate hanging open
and let that gate be the sun.
Then picture a boy bursting from the spell
of too much dark, how he tumbles
and slips from the effortless grip of the clouds.
What seemed last night like a good idea,
spanking the water.
I don't really understand why he had to die
beyond understanding the statute of limitations—
how imagination goes unsupported in the sky.
I suppose I understand how water goes on living,
while people like you and me prophesy a kind of patience
a pride in flying low, a wisdom
in the plain joy of just walking around.
But, to really understand this story
you have to imagine a kind of castle loneliness.
Nights when there is no telling
from all the things that men do, just what *we* want to do.
From that flightless dark
it is just a small step to seeing any sign of sun
as the kind of beauty our knowing can embrace.
Maybe it is just youthful infatuation,
but who wouldn't open their arms?
Who wouldn't feel in the light of such knowledge
like putting on their wings and going out?

Picture a gate hanging open.
And let that gate be the sun.

The Last of the Snow

Maybe this was your hardest year
and you turned away, like a tree
peering within its own bark.

The feeling went on forever
while snow fell in long division
falling through a screen of days.

Did you know you'd open your hand
when it was over? Would you call it love
that something, beginning again?

Now, the last of the snow
is on the ground like a soft paw
or an old trophy of the sun.

Its going has something to tell,
but what it is, is hard to say.
Though looking where it's disappearing

in patches on the ground,
you sense it's not simply that the world
wants to be new forever

but the world
if it can want anything
wants to have the *feel* of a world.

Adam & Eve

The whole world
balanced, poised and imminent like a tree.
The word introduced as proposition begins a great inventory.
Now these trees with their stronger color.
The time of year the world cries from the bough, "I owe,"
and knowing there's nothing I can do about it
I like to think about Adam and Eve
blowing it in the garden, and nothing they could do about it,
for if you've ever been in a garden and heard God's voice
you know it's too high, only dogs can hear it.
It's a nervous sound. You hear barking.
Garden junkies, I like to think of them saying over and over
"Naked, Dumb, Blind," and laughing
saying "Love Thy Snake," while God's green flower
is working its savor on their brains. Maybe knowing
from the start that they were made for fall.
Going to find out the hard way that knowledge is always
knowledge of something. Going to find out
that the inside is not the outside.

But it's the stuff about the rib that I like best.
And I picture him later looking down her blouse
and feeling like he's about to drown.
Of course no one is to blame. And when they think back
they remember the snake fondly, the character actor
who couldn't quit looking at her, whispering to itself
Give her something. The long neck. And they remember
the monotony of Paradise.

Fall, looking back and knowing change is good for the soul.
Remembering how pleased they were to find they weren't
the last people on earth.
Then going outside, and the first thing, confronting the tree.

Gulls

This one fishes old style
gathering the line hand over hand
so the wire does its thinking in a circle
in the bottom of the boat.
And what is a boat, but a wooden ditch
a small room in a sea, an opening.
A minute ago I was in the kitchen,
no baby crying, just the six o'clock in the morning
cupboardy light. Flannel blues and grays
softening up the floor and the walls.
Now it's the sharp and damp smell of gasoline
and now the sun, the full theater of the sun
torching the town, so the windows
of the houses along the shore burn like glasses of tea.
At the bottom of the bay there is a windy river
where the fish gather. When one hits
it strikes the propeller of your arm
and your hands go round like the gods of joy and labor
until the fish, most likely a cod, blinks
in the rink of light beside the boat.
All I remember is all day, hand over hand
the one, one, one. And then cleaning.
How far I had come from the city
to be there throwing the insides of fish to the gulls.
Taking from the sea and giving to the sky.
How far to find that the miserable fraternity of gulls
clawing at the air as if to be let in
made it easy to know how entitled I was
to give them as much as I wanted.
From the beautiful body of fish, as much as I wanted.

Early in the Book of Brothers and Sisters

It's early in the book of brothers and sisters.
We're crossing the lawns of the suburbs
traders on a walk through the stars.
The blue waters of dusk part for us.
The grasses turn to Persian rugs.
In one hand I carry a velvet bag
and in the other a prayer book.
Soft body of tallis calmed my small shoulders.
Simple body of prayer book kept me from flying away.

Rosh Hashonah.
I can still hear the shofar on the turnpike
can hear its stipple hit the concrete.
A horny toot sibilance, a chaos in the lives of children
men, boys, women, girls.

My memory is wrapped in that wilderness.
Wrapped in beautiful shawls, wings, drapery
in which each person is no less
than a tree, a cloud, a kind of tossing
a kind of thrown together.

If on some days all we have
is a few words to swing like a knife in the dark
on others we sway in our penumbra shawls.
Swaying in and out of our small circles
out of the small shadows of our lives.

Soon we would be returning home.
Soon we would see our house with its excited lights on.
They're blowing the shofar tonight, I say to myself
looking up at stars' bright vigilance.
Reminded how our prayers fly around like leaves
and how peace comes with anticipation.

Early in the book of brothers and sisters
I crossed the lawns of the suburbs.
In the sky our ancestors were lighting small fires.
The soft body of tallis touched my shoulders.
The simple body of prayer book
kept me from flying away.

Deer

They appear
    a draft away from the originals.
Newlyweds
    handsome as bark and leaf
        slim as grass shade.

One always seems to have a head down.
    The other hearing something that needs to be heard.
They come out of the shelving of the woods
    and stand by the door to their house.

One skips away
    as a friend once said,
ticking like a rocking horse back and forth,
    tinkering the lock between branch and bough.

When the other lifts its head, the world we share grows steady.
    Maybe that's it—they know the way to and from
from this world to the other—
    but why linger here?

I know from this one's pale look
    that it doesn't have to stir to think good thoughts.
Now it goes to join the other
    in the deep house and complicit tree.

For one quick moment, I think I will follow.
    It's something we've all wanted to do.
To fly where one love follows another,
    make a life and rise among the neat and rooted.

Yes, I say, I will go.
    I will go into the woods, if the woods will have me.

Absence

A light rain leads me.
And though I know I cannot find you
I continue past your house

and on to the farms. The last place
in the world we walked together.
The place where once a bird

grew into flame
throwing up its wings and leaving.
Nothing could make the world so still

as a bird's wings, lifting
and pushing. Nothing.
And what were our walks

but a kind of sympathy for the earth—
the fields, the trees.
Everything in that other half of the world.

It's time.
Time to admit absence.
Time to let the flowers do their work.

I cannot find you.
Even with the rain's gentle leash
I cannot find you.

Eastport

I did a dumb thing
and got carried away, out
in a small boat, in the bay
when the tide was the strongest.

If you were on shore
you might've seen me
slipping like a kite in the sky,
the tide taking twice my once.

I did then my hardest longing,
finally half closing my eyes
and chanting, rowing and chanting.
Trying to save myself

from wild crying.
Save myself. For that small boat
was a made thing.

Peninsula State Park

The smell of fire among wet pines.
The tree is sweet,
its reek beyond smolder.
Tonight our circle of stones
seals us from the woods
and the unwooded sky.
Tonight we have to wait
until ember, for the hard lights
to straighten the shoulders
cool dark to soften the bed.
For stars to divvy leaf, petal
travel down the stairwell
of each stem, each root.
The earth is turning, the pines
are the first to know.
They're wheeling in night
on the head of a pin.

Stars,
my advice is hold your places.
For though we haul with us
another day
we hardly know how
to knock on these doors
these abiding woods.
Or leave ourselves a little time
when we're not playing host.
Though it's true tonight
we seem happy, as we can only be
once in a while.
Going to the ground for sleep.
Tearing at the foot of the woods
for a little fire.

Spring Song

I know my soul will be there

in spring. When winter clouds

like great nests lie down in the ditches.

When navies of cold air

set sail and the last of the dinosaurs

crawls from the lake and melts on the shore.

And the ground begins to soften.

And to flower.

And a warm wind could wake almost anything.

Tonight the sky is crowded with stars.

And though the visible light

of all those bright suns could fit under a fingernail,

the mind is satisfied. It doesn't take much.

I know in the wind.

I know in the first green knot of spring

my soul will be there.

The Tree

Light, light as a feather.
And the little oak's neck strains
as my mother asks me, What are you doing?
Words of love slipping the undersides
of new leaves in our little backyard.
It's a thin nothing up here, that's what I'm doing.
Later, I go up the long ropes of the tree
gravitating, leaning towards
the shapelier limbs. A kind word, a word of love
or patience makes no difference.
Get down, you'll break your neck!
But I have no neck to break.
Now, the oak's neck strains a little more.
My wonderful mother doesn't know
I'm up here, in my thirty-third year.
Christ in his tree, and me in mine.
And how can I become perfect like him?
I didn't tell you to go up there, my mother says
her words trailing the miles through the backdoor screen,
they come up and skip the tree entirely.
Climbing down,
the guy next door puts on some music.
I've come home to build my mother a deck.
This is what I can give, and I turn my music on
and start to work. Standing in the backyard
after seeing my mother run into the house like a girl.
The guy next door waves to me and my mom.
Backyard to backyard, it's my music against his.
Who said we are natural on earth?

Two

The Comet

At night in Georgia
in a bed that squeaked like old magnolias
I looked up at you and felt my moorings
fall slowly back to earth.
In the morning with sand in our shoes
we drove on to Florida, driving happily
toward some doughy winter sun.
I remember pulling off the road
in the Keys at dusk, the soft murmur of the water
and the soft murmur of the road's gravelly treble.
Then getting out of the car, I dipped my head
to the dark in the dark head of a telescope.
At first, I saw nothing.
Nothing in the economy of that mind-empty dark.
And then there was something—
like a finger, or a smile
somewhere in the shutter from childhood to old age
something like desire, desire and light
sizzling in the black and blue of space.
It was January, and we'd been together four months.
Falling in love, and now looking at the comet
through thick glass, I seemed to understand
how it too might want some sun
some lovely stretch of beach to warm away a day or more
and how in its perpetual night
might start throwing off blouse after blouse.
We barely knew each other
though I suspect we felt that we could go together
slow and clumsy through a life or two.
All day, while the comet burned invisibly above
we drove toward some doughy winter sun.
That first night in Florida
you leaned against the car, looking up at the stars.
So lovely, and normal in your light.

Cyclops

of course had another eye,
but what he saw made him angry
or so it was thought.
But it was the other eye,
always trying to wake up
what already hurt
reminding him of something
out in space, for that's where
the eye was, *comet-ed,* ordained
for travel, and sped willingly
like a vowel sparring on in between
making Cyclops a little nervous
because what was really worrying him
was that long death, the one lived
before he was born, and the possibility
of stumbling on *that* in space
by some eye that was him
and only half of what was going on.
Others might prize it,
that which might come through the clouds,
make burn marks on the earth.
But vision was hard enough with one eye—
hard enough to lurch forgetful through the present—
that which comes up at any moment to blind you
to take you from the little tasks
that might be deeds.

Swimmer

I saw him going some mornings early.
Taking the small boat through its first steps.
Slowly rowing to the middle of the lake.
There was a raft, and he would go immediately in.
Arms that had done their work
around a desk, now opened like umbrellas,
fingers feeling, and the body arched like a bridge.
The sky passed over, water, and water walkers.
He'd swim well beyond the end of summer.
How slender those days were.
How quiet and resolved.
And how quietly he swam.
The sun seemed to follow
as they went around in conversation
I wanted to hear.
Though watching him from shore
I seemed to know the calm of his life,
seemed to feel it held an enduring love.
One he would have, but have to pursue.
Slowly swimming, slowly lifting his body
and continuing.
That's the way it is.
Our knowledge of others is indirect.
Though as a child, I didn't feel I needed any more
than to see him, see him going around
in daylong circles.

My father's face pressed against the face of another
and the sky reflected there.

Dream After Birth

Three inches underground
I lay on my back sleeping on fire.
A verse of flame from within
roaring from every exhausted pore.
Daylight smoke in sheets of flame
giving away my body's flume of light.

That was a few days after the birth of my son.
That was fire feeding the life to follow.

Now as I lay in the garden
and gaze at the cool and perfect sky
I can still remember the air raid of my body,
how I lay flaming, a quivering flesh.

In this simpler place
I no longer see the god of fire.

Here there are lilacs and day lilies
and the yellow eye of the daffodil
and the lipped body of the rose.

Maybe this is how it really is.
There is no flame to cure the body.
No fire to ease the soul.

Though no one could tell me
as I lay down the loose veins of my body
open in the hive of the earth
that I wasn't doing what I wanted
that I wasn't being true.

This Year the Water

Water crustaceously nursing the shore.
The body of waves rising and falling
and desire never slack.

That's it. Or to be a part of it?
Last year the ocean lifted you
and slammed you down. You roared

when the ocean roared.
You even left something like breath
on the shore.

Now you've returned
to the same ocean, sand, sky.
But today the water is too cold

and no one is going in.
It's as though you're being refused.
Though looking down the edge of sand

and water, for a moment you feel
maybe this *could* be our beginning.
The math is right, we've all been here

and like drones to an original flower
we've returned. The truth is
you have nothing to say.

Last year your heart was broken
and you sought redemption
in the big pantomime of the sea.

Now, it seems, you're feeling better
driving home in dry clothes
humming to yourself,

Mother is ice. Mother is ice.

There Were Times

There were times you thought
you were more likely to encounter God

than beauty in the form of a woman.
Were you ready to accept that?

Ready to forgo the arms of another
empty the purse of your longing and go on?

It doesn't matter. You were wrong.
When a woman opened her arms

you sang as if her breath were your own.
But maybe you were wrong about that, as well.

For what is God? What is beauty?
Yes, next time will be different.

You will use your fingernails more,
the bones of your knees

and the muscles of your ass.
Maybe even the flesh of your face,

or the blind flesh of your eyes.

Joe, 2 a.m.

Joe in his pizza doorway.
The restaurant closed, cleaned up.
Hands on hips, he's ready to go home.

Not quite ready.
The roundness of night
surveyed from his little kingdom.

Passing by I raise my hand
to call my *Buona Notte*
feeling strangely happy

proud, as if it were possible
to be proud of the god
the one who raised the first gluey words

raising audience from rain
drizzly whispers under trees
the night filling, flooding.

Imagine
before light there were only words
and the dark all inside.

Joe resident in his doorway
calls with his smaller, more experienced
two in the morning *Buona notte.*

Abandoning a Car in Brooklyn, The Thing About Angels

They called you crazy
and were so beautiful, their veins
tracing their stay on earth. Blue,
the color doesn't exist but here
in the sky like collateral.

And they came down from their apartments
and gave you gifts, helped push the car,
got dressed in their confirmation clothes
and made funny faces.

Of course they couldn't fix it so it would run
outside of their precincts. For that's the thing
about angels. They're stationed to their nooks.
And you had, therefore, to part, all smiley
and benediction

so you could continue, preparing
to abandon it and waiting, not sure if on
the next block you would be an old man
hauling a fish against the last pages of a book—
soon you could sleep, the tourists go home.

You can't be seven layers into Brooklyn
with all your toys and get involved with angels.
They steal your heart believing in you.
You who ask for everything before trying
to get it for yourself.
Who loved that car, and promised
to bust those angels out of Brooklyn
next time the world was hot on your heels
even if they don't want to go
and the spontaneity eludes and disappoints them.

End of the Season

Nights
when the fruit exists to hang

and hot as dirt days
move like boxcars pulled by flies
it seems like a year until the heat
begins a soft drift from the animals' backs
as they stand for the evening milking
and then the barn is sliced with shade
suddenly like shallower water.

I was down on the farm, pulling the last calf
from its birth-drenched mother, confident
this bull would be born in the dim
and the tame, the yellow hay of the dairy.

A block away a new house was being topped,
carpenters were beating their drums
with a steady lub-dub, socking nail
to rafter with the confidence
of judgment, that's where they belong.

That's when I left the farm,
leaving the slippy days of cows
and feed and calves behind.
Taking off with the crows and blackbirds
into the skinny heights of the tree
with those that yanked themselves up
from the low flights
to the top to wait there
for single audience with the sky.

At the end of the season
I was up on the roof of a house
able to stop for a moment and see
across to the farm

and after work
I went back, lingering
there like a stranger,
like the warmth of hello

that lingers for a while
in the higher than knee grass
the cows mouth down
to green nothing.

Islamorada

After centuries along the shore
palms have developed warm wind
as a means of sleeping beside the crush
of the waves. Now a breeze comes
like a cipher through the screens.

As tourists we're doing so many things
at once, and nothing.

Skin diving this afternoon
I held my breath and dove to retrieve a conch—
mortals in the long blue room
the ocean was holding us as if we were
thinking in another's mind—
and when I dropped the jewel,
pulling in its foot, I saw
it was an artifact to this world,
this place with enough light to read.

And then you flippered away
from our buddy system, spying on
a small gray fish attached to the side
of a larger blue, following to see
how long the marriage would last.

Sinking upward in the helpful medium
the six hundred varieties of fish seemed schooled
in visitors, dekeing and then yawning away
the way I yawn tonight, getting out of bed
to get another beer, floating
through the small honeymoon suite
to the kitchen where I pull the surf
from the top of the fridge, then back to bed
where it seems unfair—

our adventure and its blue water
closed for the night—five days
from now we'll return to the buff of winter
though now leafy poetic airs idle, musing

sometimes in January
a man can feel like a giant,
lying in bed with a beer.

I settle back to bed
in the privacy we keep around us,
kept awake by the ease of the palms,
plovers wandering the beach,
or the ease and determination of needlefish
pursuing smaller fish in the safety of the bay,
where each life is sequel to the shore.

Salvos of warm wind from the open window
roll across my chest—

> *It must be on the good days*
> *when those that are getting what they need*
> *feel for everyone—*

falling asleep, earthbound as Gulliver.

Nature

My body bends like an old glove
in the mirrors of the gym.
A stringy blue light shines on my belly.

It is winter. Brothers and sisters
move as if slugged into existence.
Is something missing? Is anything lost?

I suspect the photon
behaves the same in a light bulb
as it does in the laundered hay of the sun

and the jet of water vented from my faucet
means to my hand what it might
in the lachrymose depths of the sea.

Still, I'm not completely blind.
When the season changes I feel
grasses' green multitude intone a mortal song.

And looking out my window
these last few summer evenings
I sense the tree, that stands centered

in the long lofts and leafy hallways of the dark,
has found the body it wants to inhabit
and will not come into the house.

Bell Tower

To the young Italian men of Florence
it's all *Mamma and the bell tower.*

The heart is out of its cage,
flying up the six hundred steps.
Hands remember well how the walls lean.
How a body bends through the soft inner channel,
or how this ascent might be a second birth.

If only Florence weren't so beautiful.
One can get so drunk on art,
one can reek of history.
But today there is no other place.
It's the light at the end of the tunnel.
The calm wind that ferries you to the top
where the city opens like a jewel in God's hand.
If you believe or not, it doesn't matter.
Here you are a beginner.
Though you know more here than anywhere else.
The beauty of handling bread.
The drama of speaking to another.
The art of crawling the sidewalk on your knees.
The fundamental grace of gazing at other human beings
the way beauty deserves to be gazed at.
Not only with taking, but with letting.

Looking down from the tower,
the red clay roofs were napping in the sun.
The whole city was smiling, playing its part.
But where there is too much heaven and not enough earth,
too much air and too little stone, the heart weeps for the street.
To walk, and walk into a theater of its own,
among its own, the body of men, and the body of women.
To nominate the other, and have the other nominate you.

From the tower I could see the hills
and the small roads that divine the countryside.
You can see it all from up there.

Mamma and the bell tower.

No wonder the monks
lived on the hills outside of town
carrying their water, saying their prayers
with the city in the distance.

Siena

It's the Palio.
They're taking their horses to church.
Youths sing in the street
in a kind of gang warfare.
They wear the colors of their neighborhood.
Now one group grows louder
backing up, rearing their heads in song.
The other, a troupe in yellow and purple
won't be bettered by volume.
Their song is their song.

A few hundred years ago
the Florentines catapulted donkeys
over the high walls of Siena
to start a plague. I wasn't there
but here, now, sipping cappuccino
staring at brothers and sisters
singing at the top of their lungs.

Here, where instead of using them
for ammunition, they walk their horses
down the aisle to be blessed for a race
that will decide whose neighborhood is best.

It's such an unusual and beautiful sight.
The animals are well behaved and respectful.
Down to the sullenness of their manes
and further, down to their muscular and bare beauty—
they seem to belong here by the altar.
They fit right in with the holiness
and the terror.

They are as quiet as morning.

Manhattan Bridge

Going to show my friend
the great lights of New York City
we found a man sleeping on the bridge.
Nearby, a fire glowed as if in a passage
of its own. We didn't see the man.
Just a breath, lifting and collapsing under
a loose house of cardboard and garbage.
Just a foot extending toward the heat
as if to keep a dream of warmth awake.

When we were boys we were good.
Now we tore a few bills from our wallets
and placed them by the fire. And then
suddenly, we were down, near Chinatown
and the Bowery, and the traffic, the fire
of traffic honking in the street.
Going to show my friend the great lights.
Now we were in retreat, with nothing
nothing to worship, nothing to take home
beyond an image.

A fire.
A man sleeping on a bridge.

Bronx Park East

My grandmother gives me a glass of cold water.
I say out loud.
My uncle wants to know if it's a poem.
She's from Russia.
She gives me what I wanted.
Is it a poem?
Did she come here to give you a glass of water?
My uncle is cantankerous.
Seventy years old,
and we're sitting in the kitchen
of the apartment in which he grew up.
I wanted a glass of water,
and I wanted to say something true.
For that you have to open your mouth
and say it, and see how it sounds.
This is the apartment in which my father
and my aunt grew up.
The one from which my father and uncle left
to go into service during the war.
The same they returned to, to find their father gone.
If they wanted a glass of water
they probably got it for themselves.
I know that's what he's thinking.
They didn't wait for Grandma to push by the table.
They didn't watch her shuttle from stove
to refrigerator, to sink, and back to table.
They just went and got it.
It wasn't a poem.
This has been her home since he was a boy.
His hands on the same table for sixty years.
When my grandmother hands me the glass
I feel that I'm among them.
I'm his brother. She's my mother. She smiles at me.
I should say, On me.

The Yiddish word is kvell. You say, She kvells on me.
Though it's not something you say about yourself.
I want to say,
My grandmother gives me a glass of cold water.
And maybe reveal how she smiles at me
with all the light of her kitchen
in her well-traveled eyes.
Eyes that left Russia when she was twelve.
Eyes that left behind her mother and father
the people she loved, the acres and the hours
she spent in her home.
My uncle is cantankerous,
but that doesn't mean anything.
Sixty years in the same apartment,
people ask her how she feels.

My grandmother gives me a glass of cold water.

Genesis

I can imagine Genesis roaring in the dark.
A decent god working alone like all gods.

And the couple.
We understand their story, don't we?
Can imagine he was lonely before she came along.
From that first day they ate together and went to bed.
In the morning it was light.
Did I leave anything out?
Maybe she was cold, and he gave her his coat.

Still, the best part has to be how the world forms
out of nothing, how nothing whips itself into a stage.
I wonder if they stopped to think about that?
If they could get beyond

> *What's this hole in my stomach?*
> *What's this pain in my head?*
> *You feel good.*
> *Let me rub my neck against yours.*
> *Let me hang out in the whites of your eyes.*
> *In your breath, let me, let me live.*

I turned from a book this morning.
It was snowing outside
and there were two birds on the feeder.
First one above the other.
Then side by side.

Silent and steady, the snow
was falling as it does in history.

I thought of Genesis. I thought of love.

Dear Mozart

The Vermeer Quartet is in town.
Playing something in A major.
I am reading the liner notes, how Haydn
evolved a new approach to the quartet.
No longer was the first chair dominant,
but all four wooed and spun intimacies
of dialogue.

And I think it's that kind of thing
that I want to keep with me.
For I like the idea of conversation
becoming a gathering, and a washing over.

And how you picked this up
and like a child strong against a father
worked it better, as a kind of praise for Haydn.
And even better, as a kind of acceptance.
For life is a gift, right?

You would be pleased to hear
these four men playing so perfectly together
that it's possible to imagine the sound
as a garden, whose composition is such
that it blossoms each time one attends.

And not only that, dear Mozart,
but in your music, we hear a conversation
so beautiful, for moments I am almost sorry
it has to take place.

The Falls

Sometimes it's all very simple.
There were three days in July when it grew so hot
the whole world was thinking one buzzing thought.
And when you thought the sun would never shut its doors
a silent darkening shoved its way forward
and the people left their porches
and went into houses, if only to make believe
there might be some rest, some sleep.
Later, with everyone in bed
you slid down the curb to the creek
and up to the falls, where a mountain of water
comes down day or night, open like an all night store.
You were surprised to find thirty or forty kids there.
Some resting, some playing in the storm of the waterfall.
A girl was clinging to the rocks, the silver water
like neon on her back and legs. And a boy made of wood,
smoking a cigarette, stepped into a wall of rain.
Many were content to simply huddle on the rocks
nourishing themselves on the warm mnemonic hum
of the wet stone, or climb inch by inch
into the squinting face of the water.
Several boys jumped from the rocks into the pool
laughing when their dives were silly, laughing
when they came up wide-mouthed for air.
The water came down on them.
Crashing and smothering, until it seemed
as though the water were a tower of years, putting ashes
on the fire of their laughing, ashes on their smiles and jokes.
And when you had seen enough, you turned to walk back.
That's when you heard something.
Something roaring beyond the machine of the falls.
Something larger, quieter.
And then it was all very simple—you heard it
in the mouths of these children.
In their mouths, and the teeth of their mouths.

Three

Happiness

In a dream
I reach into a crib at night,
lean over and lift a blue silk torah
from its bed. And look!
It is my son.

Asleep or crying, I cradle him
sometimes holding his head
and rock like an old priest
in love.

As a boy,
I saw the old men pray
wrap weekend arms
around the torah
and carry their stiff baby
around the temple.
If they fell
it would mean weeks
of bread and water.
To me, a small boy,
it seemed such a risk.

Years ago,
sitting with a friend
I saw my father
standing in a field
and my friend said,
Look at that man swing!
And I watched him
in the distance—a life away.

In one of my first efforts
at poetry, I wrote
"too young to buy, I built my strength
running at my father."

It's late summer
and my son runs at me.
I can see by the yellow
and orange glass in his eyes
that he runs blindly
into day's abundant light,

and I can do nothing
but fall, and laugh with him
and hold him
and take this risk.

My son's head rests
sleeping on my shoulder.
And I know
what others have known.
And no one will blame me
if I give everything I have
to him, who runs at me—
who lets me for a while
into his dream.

My Father

Pop sees me
come back from the afterlife.
A small night table light guards
his orbiting. He's reading and says,
How was it? I'm always coming down
from my old room, looking in
taking his smile for a smile, a promise
that he won't grow old without me.
He's reading an archaeology book
and a history book. I imagine
in one there's a people who knew
a thing that was hard to look at,
and in the other, on every page
he finds that they were doing
the best they could.

When I see my father lying in bed, reading
I want to pass by and say,
Be my happy father.

Prayer Shawl

A bird will fly up on the house
and for five straight minutes tell it like it is.
Girl music and boy music.
The birds know this, and summer.

A fracas of brain cells busted
from last night's booze. And next door
Little Jim, son of Jim, is wailing
for his formula, while Dad
picks up the bass line with his drums.

The great poems of the world
sprawl on the floor. Pages fan out.
A breeze releases a little sleep. I sleep. I eat.
I dream of a summery goddess
crazy in the head, hair full blast, who walks up
and kisses me, kisses me.

Jim knocks on the door.
He's here on the east coast to play rock 'n' roll—
has six or seven beats he likes to work out on,
wants to know if I lift weights.

Dialing my mother's phone,
in the back of my mind, I want to ask her
to send my prayer shawl
as if I have the wrong one, and want my own—
but can't ask her to go upstairs to our old room
and differentiate its blues from my brother's.

Outside our bird
has reached the ridge. And is singing
what must be a song.

You Are the Hero

When a deer
steps from the trees
you stop as if to run your hand

along the curved branches of its back
the boned linen of its side, feeling such beauty
must be sister to your heart.

And you check each other
for a long time. For the deer will allow this,
will allow you to understand

there will be no break
in the silence between you.

Earlier, four people
were walking the other way
through the woods.

One smiled, another looked down,
one furtively back. No words.
This is our nature, the universe

does not adjust in the presence
of another, and we pass like sentries
in the silent cars of our thoughts.

Now, just over there
as though lifting its reflection
a doe lifts its face from the stream

and for a moment
you are like the hero in a story
who is neither surprised, nor disappointed

but understands.
There will be no break
in the silence between you.

Homage

A friend of mine left the priesthood
after twenty years. But doesn't everybody
want to drive a bus and live in the country
and have a family?
This was a long time ago, but I remember
visiting a run down mobile home
and across the way a small herd of Holsteins
chewing on nothing in their piece of the sun.
And how we worked together
painting, repairing pipes, and nailing a few steps
to the side door, which is always the front
on mobile homes.
By late afternoon we were satisfied—
until supper, when the patched together pipes burst
sopping the small pit of the kitchen.

One of the greatest things I've ever done
was simply to have the presence of mind
to run outside and shut the water.
I remember throwing my arm
up to my shoulder in the warm mouth of the earth
finding the valve, cold as an iron nerve
and turning and turning.

We all want to save someone, or something
and for a moment I was.
Though with my hand far in the earth
I began to think. I began to imagine
some uncoiling life, some swerving head
waking and knowing in its middle ear
that its lock was being picked,
and I imagined the electric slap arriving
in a kind of homage, for in homage
such decisions were made a long time ago.

When I go back there in my head
it is always dusk and darkening,
I am under a trailer
turning a small wheel in the earth.
A man appears above me, a silhouette
who watches for a moment and then turns
and goes, steady as a small star
up the three steps we made that afternoon
and into the house, and the mess, the mess
we made, the mess I think he wanted.
Going to turn on evening's first lights.

And for moments I know that if he could
he wouldn't let anything real or imagined hurt me.

One hot day in summer growing cool and dark.
One evening's small home lights
coming on the hill, like a likeness of water
dowsing to the bone.

Noah

Noah contemplates the door marked "Men"
and the door marked "Women."
Though no one else has been asked
he knows very well that he's not a great man.
Feels from the roll of the waves
that he's going to make a great witness. Famous.
Pictures himself the one who saw death float by—
bicycles, washing machines, a lot of black branches.

Noah worries that he won't be able to remember.
Starts keeping a journal. Finds himself reviewing the letters.
The characters, taking each one down from the shelf,
dusting off the consonants, oohing and aahing over the vowels.
Putting them back on the shelf.
Once a week swabbing the deck he notices the graffiti
in the women's room is always the same. ADMIT GUILT
Some kind of news that stays news.

Noah thinks about getting a tattoo. A testimony,
something to describe a day in the life.
How standing on deck at dusk a warm wind frisks the body.
Heroism Noah thinks. Or *Wind.*
Noah's gift is having no ambition.
Sits out on the deck shaving a bar of soap.
Grows sentimental about the light rain that began in his mirror.
Remembers spring, begins dreaming desperately of the bird
and the little green music.

At night thinks he hears
a woman crying in the embrace of love.
Sees the electric hips swinging his way. Can hear in the folds
of the waves the hug and moving held sigh.
Noah gets out of bed, goes to the window, and looks out
as if cool night will whisper *her* to *him.*
The dream Noah is having changes.
The sheriff comes to town and says to the villain,
"There ain't enough room in this town for both of us."

Noah writes in his journal, *"Passed death in storm
and continued sailing perfect seas."*
He likes what he has written though he thinks he'll have to
change it if anything from his former life returns—
"Should former life appear below moon and star."

And there are stars. Thousands.
Noah feels their secret pressure. Feels that the ark
can slip by. Go in this night of life unnoticed.

Day is entirely different.
Captain of a rudderless ship and his own plateau
Noah contemplates the door marked "Men"
and the door marked "Women."

Grandmother

The enamel gloss has been applied
so thick the cupboards won't close.
They've been painted by an expert of the past,
the doors are caricatures of doors.
And when the characters from my story come here,
the good cop Forget it, and the bad cop What
they're swept from the table
like the crumbs of semi sweet cookies
my grandmother pushes from one hand to the other,
scraping with the foot of her hand
again and again as if to take the table
down to bone, scrape the meat off, rub the world
back to tabula rasa. Pure white.
White, as if once upon a time there was a snow.
It covered what there was of a town,
fell into woods. Those venturing there
said it was "Beautiful." And when it had stopped
snowing there was calm, as if the snow
had fallen from the eaves of a common house,
peaceful as if it had fallen twice.
In this same kitchen my grandmother
told me a story when I was young.
A Russian story she gave me like a toy.
Ten. She had a dog. Her parents had a farm.
Like unforecasted weather the story got weird.
The dog, killed in the kitchen. Choked.
I can still hear the story. Feel the floor of the kitchen creak.
See the dog. The man who has to make his point
striding across the kitchen.
And then snow. Forgetfulness. White like loss in one's eyes.
Scraping crumbs.
Though sometimes a smile like a memory kiss
would come on her face as if the story
were about something else,
something for the eyes to be happy to travel,
tellers to tell. Hands to hand over.

These crumbs go from hand to hand. From the strong
instinct to remember to the other to forget.
Sometimes when I'd ask, she'd smile
and say the dog's name was Jilka.
Though other times Shulka.
If you pointed this out to her she'd look at you.

Who could laugh better than my grandmother?
Why else would one have children?

Holocaust Memorial, Baltimore, Maryland

Walking through Baltimore
like a city divided. Portuguese sailors
are in the harbor to honor discovery.
An old man dances with his arms in the air.
My arms ache for something to embrace
something to hold. I wander into
the shot tower, where lead was dropped
hundreds of feet from a time when war
was just a cool dark pool. I go into
a delicatessen for a drink, looking for
the dreidel of my mother tongue.
A block away in high heels a girl summons
me to her hem. Which is what she wants
to talk about—by the bar, by the bar.
I want to. I want to and I'm afraid or just
ashamed. We all want to know the warm
bell of another's body. To pull the chain
in the dark. To be simply all body.
I give the boys on the corner a few bucks.
And dollars to the couple with the carts
and the baby, and walk through the city
like a man divided.

In front of the memorial two concrete walls
come together and almost touch, leaving
a sliver of light in the space between.
Even before I read the words, before my feet
burn on the tracks, I feel I will not be able
to get through.
I write the names. The thirty-eight secrets.
The thirty-eight homes of death
beginning with Auschwitz and Birkenau
and Blezec and Bergen Belsen, to Stutthof
Theresienstadt, Treblinka, Vaivara,
and Westerbork. Putting the dark salt
in my notebook. Cataloguing the ashes
without knowing why. Just writing the words.

There are some men sitting nearby
in the shade. And now I see, they're resting
out of the glare of their poverty,
while thousands of leaves on a tree overhead
glitter like a thousand dark silhouettes.

From a tree nearby a baby bird croaks out
its first unlovely sounds. And in that
first raw noise I can almost hear
the mechanical transfer. From the vulgar
and physical, to the sublime and spiritual.
And for a moment, I know how the listener
must choose for the trick to work.

It's summer in Baltimore.
I stand in front of the memorial once more
before I molt back into my life.
On one block I sought the comforts of my body
on another the charity of my soul.

What good is a sliver of light in a wall
if I feel I will not be able to get through?

Grace

The hospital bed is a mute hand.
It has nothing to say
and cannot be improved upon.

My grandmother—Grace
was not afraid of death. And said so.
And in response

the grime of my own fear
lit a cold fire, and I shivered,
my light fallen and ashamed.

Earlier, I wondered
what we would do if we had our real work.
If this life and death were truly ours

would we lie down in the bed
in which we are going to live forever
and begin talking?

This is not for some, she said
and for a moment it was like leaning into a candle
until we were completely inside.

And how thick and luminous it is
to be in time! And wonderful
but only for a moment.

Later, I went back
into the light
in which we would be separated

and put my hands in hers.
And when they were finally warm, she said
Your hands were cold. You were frightened.

Our real work?
To die is one thing, and to live another.
And how relentless it is to love.

Rock and Water

They were a perfect pair.
The boy hunched over near the rocks.
His shadow moving gently on the surface
as if he were stirring the water.
When you looked closer, you could see
that he had something in his hand.
A small silver fish.
He was stroking it. Placing it in the water
in swimming position.
It floated to the surface and lay on its side.
Once, twice.
The sun shone on the side of the fish
and the boy continued.
Nearby another boy stood with a fishing pole
facing the other way.
He was busy and only looked over once in a while.
The boy continued trying to help the fish
by adjusting it in the water, placing it in motion.
Patiently and deliberately, as if placing the last piece
in a puzzle. As if it only needed a little help, a touch.
Once in a while the fish would actually stir on its own
and then it would slip to the surface as if having died again.
Each time the boy seemed more intent
and repeated his stroking, hovering like a guardian
repeating this ritual of patient affection and concern.
It was a very clear day. The water and the light glittered.
I stayed until I couldn't watch any longer.
Hovering as if to understand.
They were a perfect pair.
The little fish did not know how to go on living.
And the boy did not know how to let it go.

About the Author

Jerry Mirskin is the winner of the MAMMOTH books Poetry Prize. He was born in the Bronx, New York and has lived in California, Wisconsin and Maine. He has worked as a herdsman on a dairy farm, as a carpenter, and as a New York State Poet-in-the- Schools. He has published widely in literary journals and anthologies, and a chapbook of his work—bearing the title of this full-length book—was published by Camellia Press. He is currently an Associate Professor at Ithaca College. He lives in Ithaca, New York with his wife, Wendy Dann, a stage director, and his son, Noah.